SOUTH WALES BUSES IN THE TWENTY-FIRST CENTURY

VARIETY IN THE VALLEYS

Simon Ingham

The author's late grandmother, Beryl Ingham, inspired his lifelong interest in the bus and coach industry. In Simon's childhood, they would travel together on various bus routes up and down the South Wales Valleys on weekends. Favourite destinations for them both were Blackwood, Cwmbran, Abergavenny and Merthyr Tydfil, but they would sometimes trek further afield to Hereford and Gloucester and even Oxford to visit family by bus. These were great times, Nan, cherished memories of our weekends together that will stay with me forever.

First published 2020

Amberley Publishing
The Hill, Stroud
Gloucestershire, GL5 4EP

www.amberley-books.com

Copyright © Simon Ingham, 2020

The right of Simon Ingham to be identified as the Author of this work has been asserted in accordance with the Copyrights, Designs and Patents Act 1988.

ISBN 978 1 4456 9664 5 (print)
ISBN 978 1 4456 9665 2 (ebook)

All rights reserved. No part of this book may be reprinted or reproduced or utilised in any form or by any electronic, mechanical or other means, now known or hereafter invented, including photocopying and recording, or in any information storage or retrieval system, without the permission in writing from the Publishers.

British Library Cataloguing in Publication Data.
A catalogue record for this book is available from the British Library.

Origination by Amberley Publishing.
Printed in the UK.

Introduction

Around the early to mid-2000s there was a concern amongst fellow transport enthusiasts that variety, in terms of vehicle type and livery, in the passenger transport industry in and around the South Wales Valleys would decline. This was mainly attributed to the expansion of larger groups across the region. It was presumed they would opt for standardised vehicle types, therefore reducing examples of the weird but wonderful rarities that independent operators had previously acquired from new or second-hand. It was looking like the corporate liveries of the larger groups would replace local identities. To name but a few, Phil Anslow Travel was purchased by Stagecoach in South Wales in 2004, whilst French-owned Veolia Transport began its round of acquisitions by purchasing Bebbs Travel of Llantwit Fardre; Pullman, Longs and Hawkes Coaches followed. In 2006, Veolia's expansion continued through the purchase of Shamrock Travel Group which included Thomas of Barry and Wales and the Marches (ironically, Bebb Travel became the legal name of the new Veolia-owned company on about 300 vehicles). Stagecoach completed the acquisition of Gyn Williams Travel (the trading name of Crosskeys Coach Hire) in February 2006 and later purchased Islwyn Borough Transport in 2009. The early 2000s was also the growth period for low-floor buses and there was a great concern for how long much-loved step entry vehicles would last. Modern low-floor vehicles increased in great numbers, threatening the existence of Leyland Nationals and Lynxes, first generation Dennis Darts, Mercedes minibuses with various body types, Volvo Ailsa double-deckers and many more.

However, looking back at the many photographs taken over the past fifteen to twenty years, it is clear that there has been plenty of variety in and around the South Wales Valleys. Variety has been the spice of life and has manifested itself in various and interesting ways: through vehicle types, branding, advertising wraps and livery design. Some companies have disappeared, notwithstanding the test of time (e.g. Veolia Transport Cymru, who gradually abandoned most of their commercial services, as well as numerous tendered bus services, before ceasing all remaining operations by April 2012). Some re-branded companies have emerged such as Red and White Coaches (albeit relatively short lived) and Phil Anslow and Sons Coaches. New companies have appeared such as New Adventure Travel, adding unexpected variety.

This publication focuses on examples of variety in the Valleys and contributory towns and cities often incorrectly dubbed 'the Valleys' by the non-Welsh. Collectively, it will demonstrate the extent of variety there has been over the past twenty years in the south-east regions of Wales, albeit there is reference to operations that span as far west as Swansea. Whilst the majority of photographs are of exteriors, there are some interior shots at the end of the publication to show that diversity has not only manifested itself in vehicle exteriors.

However, there are many more examples of vehicle types, livery, branding and advertising, etc. that have not been mentioned. Certainly, 180 pictures are not enough to cover the amount of variety that there has been in the bus and coach industry in and around the South Wales Valleys over the past twenty or more years. Undoubtedly, the pictures will evoke memories of sightings and journeys made on examples of vehicles that have proudly served Welsh communities in the twentieth century.

If the past twenty years is anything to go by, we can expect plenty more variety as we move into the 2020s and beyond. Let's hope that operators can continue to connect people and communities with the deserved amount of local and national governmental support. Perhaps we can expect a variety of a different kind as electric, alternative-powered and autonomous vehicles emerge into the market.

Recognising eighty years since the formation of Western Welsh, Stagecoach in South Wales' Plaxton Interurban Volvo B10M R784 CDW (52504) displays its commemorative livery at the 2009 Barry Festival of Transport. It was the only one to receive such livery, standing out from others from the batch, which wore standard livery with Stagecoach Express vinyls.

Stagecoach in South Wales resurrected the Red and White name with Red and White Coaches, on the buyout of Phil Anslow Coaches in November 2004. Plaxton Interurban Volvo B10M P771 TTG (25401) is seen resting in Abergavenny bus station during May 2007. This and similar vehicles in this livery sometimes helped on Megabus services, adding variety alongside Plaxton Panthers dedicated to the coach work at that time. The 'on hire to Megabus.com' banner is just about visible in the windscreen.

South Wales Buses in the Twenty-First Century

P771 TTG is seen again but this time at Stagecoach in South Wales' Cwmbran depot, in yellow Student Link livery with sisters P772–4 TTG (25402–4). Volvo B10M-62 Jonckheere Modulo S672 RWJ (52632) sits amongst the Interurbans in the same adaptation of the corporate livery. It was new as Stagecoach East Midlands 672.

An April 2006 shot of Stagecoach in South Wales' (but new to Stagecoach Manchester) Volvo B10M, with Northern Counties Paladin bodywork. P885 MNE (20885), in Rhondda Tramways heritage livery, is seen at Rhondda Heritage Park alongside ex-Rhondda buses A14 RBL (20001), which started life as one of a pair of Alexander coach-bodied Volvo Citybus double-deckers, this one registered B176 FFS. Alongside again is step entrance Dennis Dart K97 XNY (32997), which was rebodied from a Wright Handybus after a fire in its early years with Rhondda Buses.

Optare Solos belonging to Islwyn Borough Transport, prior to takeover by Stagecoach in South Wales, resting in Blackwood bus station in October 2009. YJ05 XOU (9) poses alongside YK55 ENJ, sporting its silver and maroon livery from its days as a demonstrator with the addition of 'celebrating 20 years of serving the community' vinyls.

Cardiff Bus Scania Optare Olympus CN57 BKA (460) sporting a three-quarter advertising wrap for 'The Magical Mystery Store', Home Sense. Sister vehicle CN57 FGA (470) is behind in standard livery. These replaced Volvo Ailsas from the Cardiff Bus fleet and were the first low-floor double-deckers for the fleet.

South Wales Buses in the Twenty-First Century

Stagecoach in South Wales operated Optare Tempo YJ62 FAF (25116) in Traws Cymru livery. It pauses in wet weather in Brecon before continuing the T4 journey through to Newtown. Optare Tempos were uncommon elsewhere in the Stagecoach fleet.

A line-up of Capital Links Super Pointer Darts which were new to Cardiff Bus in 2001. Awaiting Capital Links vinyls, freshly painted Y386 GAX (386) stands alongside Y373–9 GAX, others from the same batch. These all-over orange vehicles stood out from the livery of Cardiff Bus in the city, although there were orange features on the front portion of buses in the main fleet.

First Transbus Pointer Darts CU53 AUP (42684) and CU03 BHV (42693) alongside each other at the former Swansea Bus Museum site, at Fabian Way. They wear heritage liveries for United Welsh and South Wales Transport respectively. Two other identical vehicles wore liveries for Thomas Brothers (CU03 BHW, 42694) and Llanelli & District (CU53 ARF, 42681).

Multiple demonstrators have provided additional yet short-term variety to the Welsh bus scene. Alexander Dennis Enviro200 demonstrator YX62 FDG stands on C5, in the former Cardiff bus station, in October 2013. For its time with Cardiff Bus, it was allocated fleet number 797. It also spent time with Newport Bus. Visible behind is a Greyhound vehicle awaiting its next trip to Swansea.

South Wales Buses in the Twenty-First Century

Still sporting its Arriva London livery and fleet number, VLW65, New Adventure Travel's LF02 PVN is seen on a Bassaleg School service. The vehicle would soon wear the blue/white livery of New Adventure Travel, in favour of its red London livery, uncommon in Wales, and hold the cherished registration H14 KFJ, which since appeared on other vehicles in the fleet.

Duplicate vehicles from afar add variety to the local scene when demand necessitates their use. London United's Plaxton Paragon B12B HF53 OBG waits to operate a duplicate service from Cardiff to London, on behalf of National Express, in the old Cardiff bus station. Behind is National Express' Caetano Levante FJ60 HXX, operated by Edwards Coaches, in dedicated livery for the 216 service, Cardiff to Bristol Airport. It is a replacement for the Greyhound service which ceased serving the Bristol/Bristol Airport extension in mid-2015.

First Cymru's Scania Irizar PB YN06 CGX (23323), named *Sharona*, in the iconic Greyhound livery, awaits its next journey on service 100 from Cardiff to Swansea in May 2015. YN55 PXH (23317 or *Good Golly Miss Molly*) is represented in model form in the Corgi Classic Original Omnibus range.

A May 2007 shot of Clarkes of Tredegar's Optare Solo YJ56 ASV, seen in the then yet to be completed Blackwood bus station, in Rail Linc livery, connecting Blackwood with Ystrad Mynach station. The vehicle would later pass to New Adventure Travel and be painted into their standard livery.

South Wales Buses in the Twenty-First Century

Phil Anslow Coaches, seen outside Cardiff Museum and Art Gallery on private hire work in January 2012. Leading is Sitcar Mercedes-Benz O815D, which was new to Barnes of Carlisle. Behind is Volvo B10M with Jonckheere Mistral body 935GWN, which was new to Shearings in 1999.

Newport's Dennis Trident ALX400-bodied V140 HTG (40) passes Plaxton President-bodied Dennis Trident LN51 KXV (422) at Market Square bus station, Newport. The latter was new to Metroline London as their TPL242. Both wear identical liveries yet this shot allows for a comparison of body styles, the President body being less common in the Newport fleet.

An uncommon vehicle type in South Wales, the favoured type of vehicle of this size generally being Optare Solos or short wheelbase Enviro200s. Wright Streetlite WF CN12 ARZ, here with fleetnumber '6', is participating in the Olympic Torch Relay, as its destination details. It later became 43006 with Stagecoach in South Wales, once its duties associated with the 2012 Olympics ended.

Stagecoach in South Wales CN53 HWO (34504), wearing an advertising wrap for Hutchings Hyundai in November 2012. Whilst the vehicles of this type that have operated with Stagecoach in South Wales enter high numbers, very few have received wraps to this extent.

South Wales Buses in the Twenty-First Century

New Adventure Travel's MCV Evolution YJ65 GKX leaves Newport's Market Square bus station, en route for Ringland, to the east of the city, in August 2017. It passes an identical example, showing the 'CrossCity' route branding for the N1 service. The route was withdrawn one month later but NAT registered a new X5 service between Cardiff and Ringland and use various vehicles to operate it from its Cardiff base.

Newport Bus trialled MAN EcoCity WX13 GHN during 2013. It is seen here leaving the old Newport bus station on the X30 motorway service to Cardiff. The vehicle made it into the local press due to it being fuelled by compressed natural gas, rather than conventional diesel power – one of very few vehicles to operate in Wales under this power to date.

First Wright Streetcar S40 FTR is seen outside Swansea bus station, en route to Morriston Hospital on route 4. These were phased onto the route from June 2009 and lasted just over six years. Major roadworks costing around £10 million were carried out in the city to accommodate these 'ftrMetro' vehicles. Upon withdrawal, and keeping the FTR memory alive, its registration was transferred to First Cymru's Volvo B7R Plaxton Profile CV56 AVF.

Newport Bus Plaxton Pointer-bodied Dennis Dart KU02 YUD (331) passes a sign of times gone by, preserved National Welsh Leyland National 2 BUH 240V (NS492), at the Riverfront, in Newport, in April 2018. New in 1980, BUH 240V is displaying route 73, which has been truncated over the years. Newport Bus run the Newport to Chepstow section, via Parc Seymour. KU02 YUD was new twenty-two years later as Armchair's DP1035 with dual doors.

National Express' Caetano Levante 2-bodied Volvo B11RT BX16 CHO, operated by Edwards Coaches, displays its rear wrap advertising for Philippine Airlines at the Cardiff Coach Station, Sophia Gardens. The wrap adds variety to the standard National Express livery with silver 'connecting stripes' that adorn the rear.

Alexander-bodied Bristol VRT WTG 360T (360), operating on Baycar route 6 in its smart Cardiff Tramway livery. The service is normally operated by articulated Scania Omnicitys, so the use of this heritage vehicle added satisfying variation for the summer period. The vehicle resides with the Cardiff Transport Preservation Group, in Barry.

New Adventure Travels YJ15 AOS (507) is seen on Custom House Street, in Cardiff, deputising for a T9-liveried Optare Tempo on the service to Cardiff Airport, whereby X11 route branding would not normally be seen. When new, the vehicle wore branding for the 'CrossCity' X1 service between Culverhouse Cross Tesco (south-west of Cardiff) and Pontprennau Asda (north-east of Cardiff), via Canton, which competes with a number of Cardiff Bus services.

Another shot of First Cymru's Transbus Dennis Dart SLF CU03 BHV (42693) departing Swansea bus station for Port Tennant, in November 2015. It wears maroon South Wales livery, being one of the four heritage liveries that First Cymru applied in 2014. Also in shot are ex-Cardiff Bus Plaxton Pointer Dennis Dart MPDs W167 EAX and V154 JKG, operating with Select Local Bus of Neath.

South Wales Buses in the Twenty-First Century 17

Seen outside Cardiff Castle is semi open-top N548 LHG, on the city's sightseeing tour, in December 2013. The Volvo Olympian, with Northern Counties bodywork, is operated by RATP's Bath Bus Company and was new to London Central as NV48 in closed-top form. Behind is a full open-top Ayats Bravo-bodied Volvo B7L.

First Cymru's Dennis Dart SLF Marshall Capital-bodied X78 HLR (41390), seen in Swansea bus station in March 2014. The vehicle was new to First Centrewest London as DML41390, in dual door formation, at the start of the millennium.

Volvo Olympian, with Northern Counties bodywork, N344 HGK (16444) was one of the last high-floor double-deckers to operate for Stagecoach in South Wales. It is seen in Pontypool, on the Tuesday, on the X20 service towards Abergavenny in October 2013. Two Optare Solos follow behind on different services, the front most example carrying the modified version of Stagecoach corporate livery with less blue on the front.

Cardiff Bus Scania-engined Optare Olympus CN57 FGD (472) in pink and orange heritage livery. Turning from Westage Street onto Castle Street, it operates on service 30 towards Newport. Interestingly, the 30 holds the title of being the last such jointly run route by two municipal operators in Britain. Apart from this livery, the vehicle has also worn standard fleet livery, a grey variant to promote the city's Iff card and red/blue livery to promote the city's sporting prowess.

First Cymru's T629 SEJ (42329), a Dennis Dart SLF with ALX200 bodywork, exits Swansea bus station on route X5 to Glynneath. It previously wore route branding for what was known as the 'purple line', service 25, Swansea to Blaenymaes.

Cardiff Bus CN06 GDY (619), sporting its generic bendy bus livery, on route 6, at Cardiff Bay, in June 2013. This was one of two to receive this livery, the other being 618. However, both lost this livery in favour of standard Cardiff Bus livery upon refurbishment at Hants and Dorset Trim.

Edwards Coaches operated Volvo B9R Caetano Levante FJ12 FXZ on National Express services with a rear wrap denoting its Welsh identity, hence its nickname being 'The Dragon'. It is seen outside Penarth Pier, having made a diversion there after showcasing its wheelchair accessible credentials at a local school. Newer Levante 2 and Levante 3 tri-axle variants have largely replaced the older twin axles.

Dennis Dart SLF Plaxton Pointer SPDs CE02 UVP (398) and CN53 ANF (T518) are seen alongside each other at their home at Cardiff Bus Sloper Road Depot. 518 once wore a black based all-over wrap advertising St David's Hall in the city. Its training livery comprises of a mainly yellow front and rear with grey sides, making it and other training vehicles stand out from the front-line operational fleet. Note the 'D' plate – the 'D' stands for *dysgwr*, Welsh for 'learner'.

Cardiff Bus CN06 GDF (601) in the earlier Baycar livery at Cardiff Bay in front of the Dr Who Experience. When new, 601 was displayed to shoppers in Queen Street, in the city centre. Cardiff Bus were recognised for the Baycar service at the Chartered Institute of Logistics and Transport, Wales' National Transport Awards, in 2007 after service 6 saw a 55 per cent increase in passenger numbers since its introduction a year earlier. Besides Swansea, Cardiff is the only Welsh city to have operated articulated vehicles.

Unusual in the national Stagecoach fleet, Caetano Nimbus-bodied Dennis Dart SLF X191 FOR entered the Stagecoach Wales fleet upon the takeover of Glyn Williams Travel and was renumbered 33291. It was named *Dean* in the Glyn Williams fleet and carried fleet number 1. Similar vehicles, X192 FOR and HX51 LRZ, were similarly painted into Stagecoach livery upon the takeover of the independent.

Newport Bus V35 HTG carried a Christmas livery and festive message to customers during 2011. Its tyres were also painted white but did not retain their colour for long, not helped by the wet Welsh weather. The livery was sponsored by various companies, including Alexander Dennis and Scania. When new, this six strong fleet of ALX400 Dennis Tridents carried a large vinyl of the Newport Wave on their side. V39 HTG is represented in model format by Creative Master Northcord Ltd.

Harris Bus's new Optare Solo SRs await their next duties alongside each other, when nearly new at Blackwood bus station, in January 2017. YJ66 ARU and YJ66 ARX are numbered 37 and 38 respectively, the latter being named *Jack*, after the founder of the company. All-over sky-blue Optare Solo SR YJ16 DDA and all-over orange YJ64 DWD were loaned demonstrators prior to the arrival of these. Another Optare Solo SR in the Harris fleet is YJ10 EXW, which was new to People's Bus of Liverpool as their Y1 BUS.

Older Optare Solos in the Harris Coaches fleet, pictured in Blackwood bus station, in April 2015, are YJ51 JWY (01), new to Thorpes as their OSL1, and YG02 FWJ (02), new as a demonstrator for Optare having spent a short time with Cardiff Bus. Cardiff Bus purchased none of the type, however examples of this type have been plentiful in the South Wales Valleys.

An October 2013 shot of Peakes of Pontypool's Town & Country Bus ALX200-bodied Dennis Dart Y241 FJN (new to Stagecoach London), as it prepares to depart Monmouth bus station on service 60 to Newport, via Raglan and Usk. Following behind is Chepstow Classic Bus-owned Alexander Sprint-bodied Mercedes-Benz 709D L329 YKV (new to Stagecoach Midland Red South) on service 65 to Chepstow, via Trellech, as detailed on the paper destination in the windscreen (nearside), due to the main display not working.

During August 2016, Newport Bus Enviro200 YX61 DVU (308) is seen on service 60 at the Square, in the picturesque town of Usk, which is the regular winner of Wales in Bloom. On leaving Usk, the service would follow the River Usk and Monmouthshire countryside to the Roman town of Caerleon. Newport Bus also operate some longer wheelbase variants of the Enviro200.

Both operated by Edwards Coaches for National Express, Caetano Levante-bodied Volvo B9R FJ11 GMY, heading to Cardiff, Bridgend, Port Talbot and Swansea on the 201 service, passes newer Caetano Levante 3-Bodied Volvo B11RT BU18 OTM, heading to London Victoria on the 509 service. This July 2018 shot allows for a direct comparison of the Levante 1 and newer Mk 3 body styles.

Swansea Park and Ride ADL Enviro300 vehicles, parked together at Swansea Bus Museum, provided a colourful composition in May 2014. SL63 GBZ (67437) exemplifies the orange Fforestfach Park and Ride livery; SL63 GBV (67434) exemplifies the blue livery for Fabian Way Park and Ride; and SL63 GBO (67432) exemplifies the green Landore Park and Ride livery. 67437 would later receive Traws Cymru livery for the T1 service operating between Carmarthen to Aberystwyth.

Cardiff Bus Enviro200 MMC CN17 BGK is heading towards Radyr on service 63, even though it carries branding for the H59 between Cardiff East Park and Ride and the Heath Hospital. Carrying fleet number 551, it is the first, numerically, from the batch of ten delivered new in 2017. Coming in the opposite direction, and carrying multi-route branding for services 21, 23, 24 and 25, is CN53 AKZ (510), on an inbound 24 service from Llandaff and Whitchurch. It formerly carried branding for services 57/58 when in the former Cardiff Bus livery.

New as Stagecoach Grimsby Cleethorpes' 671, Stagecoach Wales' Jonkheere Modulo-bodied Volvo B10M-62 S671 RWJ (52631) is witnessed at Chepstow whilst being used on service 14, in March 2012. In 2016, it was repainted into School Link yellow livery, alongside native Plaxton Interurbans and other Jonkheere Modulos.

Seen exiting the old Cardiff bus station, on the X40 service to Aberystwyth in April 2007, is Arriva Cymru-operated Optare Tempo YJ55 BKK (2861), which is displaying the Arriva version of the Traws Cambria livery.

South Wales Buses in the Twenty-First Century

Sightings of vehicles from Edwards Coaches are pleasant and common across South Wales. Seen outside their Swansea depot in March 2014, during an open day, are Neoplan Starliners PK62 VUX (in standard livery) and ML13 XOB (in Team Wales red livery). ML13 XNZ is another Starliner in the Edwards fleet and wears standard livery.

A pleasant photograph of variety in the old Blackwood bus station in October 2005. Note that no large operators are in shot but buses from three independents and one from the then smallest municipal bus operator, Islwyn Borough Transport, are. 'The bus that meets the train', Clarkes Coaches Mercedes-Benz 709D P684 HND rests between duties on the RL5. Alongside are Harris Coaches' step entry Dennis Dart J127 DUV, Glyn Williams Travel's Caetano Nimbus-bodied Dennis Dart X192 FOR (12) named *Steve* and Islwyn Borough Transport's ex-Tillingbourne Optare Vecta TIL 5405 (30).

Operating on service 7 to Pontyprydd is Veolia Transport Cymru's Mercedes-Benz Vario R103 TKO (new to Arriva Kent and Sussex), in May 2007. Veolia did not remain a major player in the South Wales bus industry scene and all services were abandoned by April 2012. Various body types were operated by the group.

Resting at Blackwood bus station are Islwyn Borough Transport's MCV Stirling AE04 PJU (22) and PN03 OWA (18). The latter was new to Stagecoach and, ironically, made it back into Stagecoach ownership when IBT was purchased in November 2009. Like AE04 PJU, it received Stagecoach corporate livery.

South Wales Buses in the Twenty-First Century

Stagecoach in South Wales' Enviro200 MMC YX67 VAJ (29193), seen operating on Gold service 120 to Blaencwm and Blaenrhondda at Caerphilly. This batch of vehicles moved from Porth to Blackwood depot for use on the 151/26 service during May 2019.

Stagecoach in South Wales' ADL Enviro300 CN60 CVO (27695) enters Newport bus station fully loaded from Blaenavon, Pontypool and Cwmbran on the X24, for which it is branded, following a downpour in October 2013. The batch assisted in London during the 2012 Olympics; legislation meant that their fleetnames needed to be covered but route branding remained.

Newport Bus Alexander Royale-bodied Volvo Olympian P279 PSX (279) is seen operating on a Newport school contract. These were a surprising transfer from Lothian Buses, being high floor vehicles with dual doors. Besides school services, they operated on main services with traditional destination roller blinds and in dark green and white livery, with black bumpers following the lines of Lothian's livery. ALX400 Dennis Trident V37 HTG (37) also received this livery.

Newport Bus operated a sizeable fleet of Scania Irizar school buses. YN04 AFU is one example, being numbered 19 in the fleet. A month later it would pass to Turners of Bristol, who retained the 'Skool' and 'keeping an eye on school safety' vinyls. Scania Omnicity YN07 VCL (49) passes in this April 2013 shot.

Arguably a Dennis Dart with an identity crisis, CE02 UVG (390), with a hybrid Cardiff Bus/Capital Links livery but with the latter's fleetnames, is seen in the Sloper Road depot of Cardiff Bus in April 2018. Note the 'On Hire to Vale Bus Lines' board in the windscreen for use on services registered under this company.

Globe Coaches of Aberaman Optare Solo YJ05 XMX, in Aberdare bus station, in July 2019. Note the 'please support your local bus service' wording on the cove panels in attempts to entice people from their cars in Valley towns. It is seen with a backdrop of Stagecoach in South Wales Optare Solos, common in the town.

Mercedes minibuses were common amongst the Stagecoach group and many were operated within the South Wales division before the advent of low floor and subsequent replacement by Optare Solos. New to GMS Buses (the only vehicles delivered new to GMS), and after passing to Stagecoach Manchester, South Wales received N425 WVR (41425), as well as others from the same batch, and operated them in various depots across the region. These had automatic gearboxes, whereas the native South Wales examples were manual. Notably, 414, one of the last operational in public service, became a staff shuttle bus (in plain white with Stagecoach fleet names). Similar 402 passed to Glamorgan Bus.

Edwards Coaches operated Optare Tempo SR demonstrator GY12 GYK on their 400E service to Gwaunmiskin from Cardiff. Edwards dropped their 'E' suffix from local bus services once competition from First and Veolia Cymru dissipated. Noteworthy at the time of photographing (March 2013) was the ability for the destination blind to be displayed in various colours. This was new technology at the time, standing out from the standard commonplace all-orange blinds.

Edwards Coaches trialled short wheelbase Alexander Dennis Enviro200 MMC YX17 NXA during August 2017. Edwards Coaches purchased six new Enviro200 MMCs in early 2019 (YW68 PCX–Z, DK/O/U), which entered service in white before being painted in fleet livery. Compared to the previous pre-MMC Enviro200s Edwards operated, the new MMCs are lighter, feature stop-start technology (reportedly making them up to 35 per cent more economical) and have an additional five seats and a redesigned interior layout.

Monmouthshire County Council-owned Alexander Dennis Enviro300 SN06 JVW has a seating capacity of sixty-one, making it perfect for school contracts, though the company mainly operates coaches. Cardiff Bus operate similar vehicles with this early Enviro300 body style. Some in the Cardiff fleet received all-over BMI baby advertising and luggage racks for use on the X91 to Cardiff Airport.

Examples of Plaxton Pointer/Transbus/Alexander Dennis Darts came to Wales from other divisions of the Stagecoach group to replace older buses within the fleet. Still wearing route branding from its time with Stagecoach in Merseyside, PX55 EEV (34764) loads customers in Blackwood bus station before starting on the 151 to Newport on a wet December day in 2009.

Edwards Coaches trialled Optare Versa demonstrator YJ61 JHF during February 2013. It is seen awaiting time on Greyfriars Road before heading back to Gwaunmiskin. The vehicle was later purchased by Lugg Valley Travel and painted into their own livery. Although Optare Versas were rare with independents, both First and Stagecoach operated them in South Wales, albeit in relatively low numbers.

Wright Streetlite DF ERZ 2028 was demonstrated with Cardiff Bus, during February 2013, in all-over silver livery, and was allocated fleetnumber 798 for the duration of its stay. It is seen operating on service 29B to Llanishen.

Operated by First Cymru, when this picture was taken in October 2013, Optare Tempo YA13 AAF (64507) is in Cardiff Airport Express livery. Over the years, the T9 service has come under scrutiny due to low patronage, with some labelling the service a 'ghost train'. The vehicle passed to New Adventure Travel when they were awarded the T9 contract in August 2014.

Once a common sight in the South Wales Valleys, Stagecoach in South Wales' Alexander PS-bodied Volvo B10M R792 DHB (20392) returns to Newport on the 64 service from Underwood, via Langstone. This shot was taken in March 2013, prior to returning to the Stagecoach striped livery that it wore when new and that it maintains in preservation at the Cardiff Transport Preservation Group.

The Champions League Final, held in the Principality Stadium, brought additional vehicle variety to South Wales when extra vehicles were required for football shuttles. Reading Buses provided support. Enviro400 SN11 BRX, in heritage livery, heads a line-up of newer Enviro400 MMCs on Cathedral Road, Cardiff.

A May 2009 shot of Glamorgan Bus Volvo B6 M423 PVN, with Alexander Dash bodywork, preparing to start service 94 to Aberdare from Merthyr. The vehicle was new to OK Travel, Auckland, in 1994.

Stagecoach in South Wales operated Traws Cymru-liveried vehicles YJ55 YGC (25103) and newer YJ62 FAF (25116). Both await use alongside each other, at Merthyr Tydfil, in October 2013. 25103 was new in the red/blue variation of the Traws Cambria livery and carries the earlier Optare badge and larger fleet numbers.

Silverline's Optare Solo S253 KNL is seen in Merthyr Tydfil bus station about to operate service 999 to Dowlais. Dowlais was once home to the Dowlais Iron Company, which employed up to 7,000 people, making it the largest ironworks in the word during the eighteenth/nineteenth century. The vehicle was new to Go North East as their 453 in 1998.

A number of former Glyn Williams UVG Urbanstar-bodied Dennis Dart SLFs received Plaxton Pointer fronts under Stagecoach ownership. The first to enter service in its new guise was R422 AOR, in May 2007. It is seen here on route 56 to Tredegar, via Markham, yet to receive its new destination equipment.

Phil Anslow built up a sizeable fleet of Alexander Dennis Enviro200s over recent years. MX13 BAA was new to South Wales Transport of Neath during March 2013. It is seen in front of similar YX14 RZB, new to G. & J. Holmes, Clay Cross, in May 2014. Both are resting on St David's Road, in Cwmbran, during September 2019. Whilst their side fleetnames differ, both, like others in the fleet, carry identical 'getting you there with money to spare' and 'low fares better value' vinyls.

Sporting its yellow 172 route branding for the service between Aberdare and Porthcawl, via Maerdy Mountain Road, is Stagecoach in South Wales' Scania-engined Enviro300 CN12 AWH (28637). The vehicle previously wore a different version of route branding for the arduous 172.

Scania-engined Caetano Levante tri-axle FJ08 KMK is seen, in February 2014, loading for a winter mini break to Oxford and Windsor. It was unique when with Veolia Birmingham, being the only Levante allocated there for National Express duties when outstationed at Astons, Worcester, for the 444 service. The large vinyls make its Welsh identity unmistakeable.

Working service 60 to Aberdare, via Mountain Ash, is Stagecoach in South Wales' Optare Solo SR CN13 CZF (47859), albeit carrying route branding for Aberdare Connect services 6/7/8/9.

Thomas of Rhondda's Enviro200 YY66 WDR (173), sporting its local link branding on service 173 to Clydach Vale, seen in Tonypandy bus station, July 2019.

Volvo B10M Van Hool Alizee M420 VYD was new in 1995 to Bates, Appledore, and passed to Netwton's of Newbridge. Others from this fleet retained their livery with their fleetnames being replaced. It is seen on a private hire, in Cardiff, in June 2016. Other vehicles in the Newton's fleet received liveries inspired by Bates, such as ex-Oxford Bus and Stagecoach in South Wales Volvo B10B Plaxton Verde P636 FFC.

Very unusual vehicles to make it into Stagecoach ownership, and be used in South Wales, were former Glyn Williams Travel BMC Falcons. In store at Bulwark depot, still wearing its former owner's livery (without fleet names), but with Stagecoach fleet number 29706, was CN04 RFZ. Alongside was similar but recently painted CN04 XCL (29708). Interestingly, sister vehicle CN04 XCK became an advertising unit for Peugeot with a 3008 Crossover secured to its roof for publicity purposes, prior to returning to PCV use with Baines Coaches of Oldmeldrum.

The early Severn Express livery is seen on First's Wright Gemini-bodied Volvo B7TL WX56 HKA (32685). These vehicles, which started life in Leeds, were replaced with new ADL Enviro400 MMCs in a refreshed Severn Express livery in 2016.

Resting, not in service, in the layover area at the former Cardiff bus station are Enviro300s CN04 NPV (701) and CN04 NRK (712) in the Cardiff Bus fleet.

Stagecoach in South Wales' Optare Versa CN57 BZA (25214) is pictured operating Sunday service X17 to Cardiff, when nearly new in May 2008. Fourteen out of sixteen of the batch received branding from new for the 151 service. Some of the batch received Cummins engines prior to transfer to other parts of the Stagecoach group.

New Adventure Travels Enviro200 CN13 EHE moves out of Pontypridd bus station to begin operation of the 103 service to Oaklands in October 2013.

An October 2012 shot of New Adventure Travel's MCV Evolution CN07 FSC, showing its 'Holby Line' branding for use on the set of the BBC's medical drama, *Casualty*, filmed in Wales since 2011.

Stagecoach in South Wales' Optare Solo CN56 EYR (47380) leads identical CN56 EYW (47385) in Tredegar. Both were only a few months old in April 2007. Both wore 'go travel' branding for Blaenau Gwent town services.

Line-up of preserved Cardiff Bus vehicles in their former home, at Sloper Road depot. Whilst the vehicles and livery are not as common on the streets of South Wales as they once were, they add pleasing variety and a sense of nostalgia when they attend rallies and running days across the region.

Alexander Dennis Enviro300-bodied Scania Demonstrator YN62 AAK with Newport Bus, in December 2012. It also spent time with New Adventure Travel and further north with Express Motors during its stay in Wales. The vehicle became a permanent member of the Midland Classic, Burton-on-Trent, holding fleet number 21.

Native to Wales in the Stagecoach in South Wales fleet, and with manual gearboxes, N375 PNY (40575) stands in front of N381 PNY (40581) in April 2006. These minibuses were gradually replaced by shorter length and low floor Dennis Darts (with Plaxton Pointer and Alexander ALX200 bodywork) and later Optare Solos.

Identical Stagecoach in South Wales Optare Solo SRs YJ56 ESN and YJ65 ESO (47975–6) in Cwmbran bus station. These made it to South Wales from Warwickshire, in October 2018. They were the second batch of Gold Optare Solos to work route G1. 47975 was working alongside the larger and dedicated Gold specification Enviro300s on the X24, a relatively uncommon working.

YT13 YUK on demonstration with Newport Bus. Seen on service 8 to Ringland, during September 2013, it is powered by compressed natural gas, a relatively new concept at this point in time and uncommon to the Welsh bus scene. The vehicle was later showcased by First as their 'Bio-Bus' with vinyls with appropriate imagery and the wording 'powered by your waste for a sustainable future.'

In support of Movember, to raise money and awareness of testicular cancer, Newport Bus applied various moustache designs to their buses during 2012. Scania Omnicity YN54 AOF (46) is one example, adding unexpected variety to the fleet.

First Cymru's Alexander Dennis Enviro200 YX13 AFE (44557) also made a rare appearance at a Stagecoach Depot at their Cwmbran Depot open day. It wears modern Western Welsh/Gorllewin Cymru fleet names and lettering. The vehicle has been based at Swansea Ravenhill depot and Ammanford sub-depot. Previously, it wore First corporate livery, as well as a three-quarter advertisement for Heart Radio. 'Western Welsh' is the resurrected fleetname for First's rural Carmarthenshire and Pembrokeshire operations. 'Swansea and the Bay' has been adopted for the area of Greater Swansea.

Although not operated in this livery, Newport's MAN-engined Wright Meridians were delivered in their former green/creme corporate livery. Two unidentifiable examples from the batch stand alongside each other when new, in January 2010.

Veolia Transport Cymru's Plaxton Centro-bodied Volvo B7RLE CN07 HVH exits Swansea bus station on service 116 to Llanrhidian Cross, in January 2011. On the demise of Veolia, along with others, this vehicle passed to First Midland Red, where it was branded for the half-hourly X50 between Worcester and Evesham. Whilst Plaxton Centro's became less common, Easyway operated VDL SB200 YJ58 FFD (ST58 FAG) and New Adventure drafted in MAN-engined KX58 BHV and KX58 BJE to support with local services.

Veolia Transport Cymru's Plaxton Primo CN57 EFH is seen in Abergavenny, on town service 43, in April 2010. Plaxton Primos were originally intended to replace the Beaver (built on Mercedes-Benz Vario chassis), but pressure from smaller operators persuaded Plaxton to continue that model. It did not fare well against the Optare Solo, which continued to sell in high numbers in Wales.

This Mercedes-Benz Citaro is seen operating on the X1 service when on demonstration with New Adventure Travel, in June 2019. It was working the service, alongside Optare Metrocitys as well as Citaros owned by New Adventure Travel, in two-tone metallic blue livery.

Newport Bus Scania Omnicity YV03 PZS (62) displaying its rear end 'we will remember them' vinyl. Various buses from the Newport fleet received the same wrap and lasted for many years. Some buses in the fleet were named in memory of soldiers who were Newport Corporation employees.

Basking in the Welsh sun on Castle Street in May 2019. On route 58 to Pontprennau, unbranded Cardiff Bus Mercedes-Benz Citaro CN65 ABX (126) passes Alexander Dennis Enviro400 MMC CN65 AAE (301) on service 44 to St Mellons, ironically branded for Pontprennau services 57/58.

Stagecoach in South Wales' Mercedes-Benz Sprinter City BP16 UWN (44001) on service 152 to Hendreforgan, in July 2019. It was new to the Stagecoach East Kent division for the pioneering 'Little and Often' network in Ashford. Similar vehicles from the same batch moved to other Stagecoach subsidiaries, some receiving standard fleet livery.

Edwards Coaches was one of many operators to trial Mercedes-Benz Citaro BF60 OEZ in South Wales. It is seen preparing to operate the 400E from Greyfriars Road in Cardiff in April 2013, with two paper destination signs in place of the electronic display.

The first-place winning design of the National Express Colour the Coach competition, showing the Wales Millennium Centre, was applied to Volvo B11RT Caetano Levante BX16 CHV, operated by Edwards Coaches.

Heading towards Blaenavon on the X24, Stagecoach in South Wales' Alexander Dennis Enviro300 SN65 ODY (27218) passes Optare Solo YJ65 ESN (47975), heading in the opposite direction. The November 2018 photo demonstrates the Gold variety that Cwmbran depot occasionally offer on the service normally operated solely by the larger Gold variant.

Modern buses to attend the Barry Festival of Transport in 2019 included Mercedes-Benz Citaro CN17 FZS (131), from Cardiff Bus, and Optare Solo YJ65 ETA (47980), from Stagecoach in South Wales. Both vehicles promote contactless payment on the rear, not heard of on Welsh buses at the beginning of the twenty-first century.

Stagecoach in South Wales CN54 ECT (34673) on a training duty from Blackwood depot. The red-based training livery, worn here, is similar to the early 2000s Stagecoach in London 'rear swoop' livery. When new, this Dart was part of a batch based at Caerphilly depot and wore standard livery with 'just go' vinyls for Caerphilly/Cardiff services A and B. Internally, it displayed artwork on coving panels produced by schoolchildren as part of Stagecoach's 'My Caerphilly' competition.

In its later life, P885 MNE passed to Newton's Travel of Newbridge. Primarily used on school services, it joined other ex-Stagecoach vehicles purchased by Newton's for the same purpose. It is seen in Swansea in June 2016.

Stagecoach in South Wales' T588 SKG Mercedes-Benz Vario with Plaxton Beaver 2 bodywork was new to Phil Anslow Travel in July 1999. It is seen in Chepstow, wearing Stagecoach corporate livery, on tendered service 761 (Beachley to Chepstow via Sedbury), later operated by James Bevan. The vehicle later passed to Lloyds Coaches, Machynlleth.

Plaxton Super Pointer-bodied Dennis Dart SLF Y381 GAX (381), wearing full Capital Bus Lines livery, in December 2016. It is seen on Westgate Street on service 64 to the Heath Hospital. The vehicle, like other Dennis Darts from Cardiff, later passed to Catch22 Bus of Blackpool. Sister vehicle Y377 GAX resides with the Cardiff Transport Preservation Group.

Freshly repainted in Stagecoach livery is CN53 GWO (29707), seen in August 2006, on service 56 to Blackwood. It was one of six similar vehicles new to Glyn Williams Travel and later passed to MacEwan's Coach Services, Dumfries.

Mainline of Gilfach Goch, Porth, operate a number of Scania K400EB4/Irizar PBs, including YT12 RMX. It is seen in Cardiff bus station prior to operating service CF1, on behalf of National Express, to the Cheltenham Festival in March 2012.

A guest appearance was made by partial open-top Wright Gemini-bodied Volvo B5TL BV17 CTO (13804), from the Cumbria & North Lancashire fleet, during the Cwmbran Depot open day, to commemorate the ninetieth anniversary of Western Welsh. Alongside heritage vehicles, it provided tours around Cwmbran town, some 250 miles away from its usual operating territory. It is only one of thirteen such examples with Stagecoach and thus brought pleasant variety to Cwmbran during its short stay.

Zeelo-liveried Mercedes-Benz Tourismo BF61 HCL, operated by Creigiau Travel, is seen at the 2019 Barry Festival of Transport. The vehicle is one of two used for the Newport–Bristol commuter service, introduced in May 2019. Alongside are preserved ECW Bristol LH6L OJD 54R and East Lancs/Greenway-bodied HLZ 4439, which began life as Leyland National GCY 748N with South Wales Transport.

First's Alexander Dennis Enviro400 MMC YX66 WKR (33929) is seen making an appearance on the Severn Express at Newport, adding an unusual sprinkling of variety as it covers for a similar vehicle with dedicated route livery. It passes Newport Bus Dennis Trident LR52 LYC (438) with East Lancs Myllennium bodywork, an uncommon combination in Wales and one of only two examples in the Newport fleet, the other being LR52 LWF, which temporarily operated in the red-based livery of its former owner, CT Plus, prior to repaint into green.

Capital City red livery on Cardiff Bus articulated Scania Omnicity CN06 GFJ (613) turning out of its home at Sloper Road depot, when nearly new in July 2006.

Without an overall advertising wrap, native CN53 HWY (34511), from the Stagecoach Wales fleet, waits time in Cardiff bus station, prior to completing another 132 journey towards Porth, for which it has subtle route branding.

Edwards Coaches' Optare Excel R209 DKG is seen at the 2013 Barry Festival of Transport. New to Cardiff Bus in 1998, it passed to Edwards from Eastbourne Buses for use on their local bus network. Standing alongside is preserved Islwyn Borough Transport GAX 137W (37), a Leyland Leopard with Marshall bodywork.

A reminder of times gone by as two Leyland Lynxes pose side by side at the 2019 Barry Festival of Transport. Exemplifying the Lynx variety in the preserved passenger transport scene in South Wales, J267 UDW (267) has Mk 2 bodywork, whilst G258 HUH (258) holds the former original Lynx styling. The latter was retained for use as a driver training vehicle after coming out of revenue-earning service with Cardiff Bus.

First Cymru Clipper vehicles, with different body styles but similar purple and gold livery, were displayed at the Swansea Bus Museum open day in 2014. From left to right were Wright Streetlite Max SN14 DVG (63091), Optare Versa YJ13 HLU (49302), complete with red bow, and Wright Eclipse Urban CU08 AHX (69305), which previously wore dedicated Landore Park and Ride livery.

Newport Bus CN60 FBV (102), seen turning out from the bus station onto Usk Way, in July 2013. This was the livery that the batch wore when first operated in Newport, despite being delivered in the company's previous green and cream livery.

New Adventure Travel's ADL Enviro300 SN09 CGX visited many operators across the UK as a demonstrator in its early years, including Newport Transport. It is seen here in Newport whilst operating the Free Shuttle to the city's Sainsbury's store. It arrived at New Adventure Travel in National Express West Midlands livery and operated in these colours prior to receiving fleet livery.

Islwyn Borough Transport's Marshall Capital-bodied Dennis Dart N671 CLV (34), seen wearing dedicated Asda Free Bus livery for use between the town's bus station and the Asda store. The vehicle became 32939 in Stagecoach ownership but is seen with Islwyn Borough Transport in October 2009.

After wearing Islwyn Borough Transport's corporate livery, IBT's N673 CLV (35) wore a revised Asda Rider livery. Upon Stagecoach's takeover, it was renumbered 32940 and would later become a staff shuttle vehicle in all-over white, like sister vehicle 32939. Both were new to Halton Transport in 1995.

Newport Bus Scania Omnicity YN57 FZV (3) in their earlier 'traditional' fleet livery in June 2010. It is preparing to operate service 28X to Caerleon, posing in front of Newport City footbridge, which linked the east bank of the River Usk, in the vicinity of Rodney Parade stadium, to University Plaza, on the west bank.

Easyway hold many personalised registrations including BW51 BUS, shown here on an Optare Solo. It is operating to St Fagans on the service for which it wears dedicated branding, the 32a. A registration that is appropriate for this specific route is ST58 FAG, which has appeared on a number of vehicles in the fleet over time.

South Wales Buses in the Twenty-First Century

Showing service 130 to Blaenrhondda on its destination, Stagecoach Wales' Dennis Dart K97 XNY (32997) is seen displayed at the Rhondda Heritage Park. It was one of the last to operate in the striped Stagecoach livery and provided cover at Stagecoach's Pontllanfraith depot, after the takeover of Glyn Williams Travel.

Stagecoach in South Wales' mini Pointer Dart T603 DAX (33287) passes UVG Urbanstar-bodied Dennis Dart S787 NRV (33282), formally named *Tom*. Both were new to Glyn Williams Travel, the former in a silver-based livery to celebrate their twenty-fifth operating anniversary. The latter was not to receive a new Plaxton Pointer front, unlike some Urbanstars from the Glyn Williams fleet.

VR Travel's Jonckheere Mistral-bodied Volvo B10M-62 was new to Brent Thomas in March 1998. Later registered TSV 497, and prior to buyout by New Adventure Travel, the vehicle rests in Merthyr Tydfil bus station alongside Stagecoach in South Wales' Alexander PS-bodied Volvo B10M P318 EFL (20698), which later passed to John's Travel. The vehicle joined many more Alexander PSs in the Stagecoach in South Wales fleet, being originally new to Stagecoach Swindon and District.

Stagecoach in South Wales' Alexander PS-bodied Volvo B10M P317 EFL (20697) was painted into Asda Rider livery at Blackwood depot and spent a short while on the free town shuttle service.

Stagecoach in South Wales' Wright Streetlite WF CN12 ASU (43008) displays a rear advert for the Brecon Mountain Railway, which service 35 serves every fifteen minutes from Merthyr Tydfil. The sides carry Merthyr town service branding.

Stagecoach in South Wales' Scania-engined Enviro300 YN15 KFV (28726) exemplifies the batch used primarily on X3/X4 services from Cardiff. It is seen leaving Pontypridd bus station in June 2019, heading for Brynmawr, via Merthyr Tydfil. Vinyls applied promote the free WiFi, plug sockets and high-backed seats that the vehicles offer, contributing to stress free travel.

New Adventure Travel's Caetano-bodied MAN City Smart OU14 SVW (340), heading from Pontypridd bus station to Nantgarw on service 102 in June 2019. The vehicle at this time had an all-over wrap promoting David Spear Vans of Cardiff and Tredegar.

With 'town link' 102 service branding, New Adventure Travel's Optare Metrocity YJ65 EWE heads towards Glyncoch in June 2019.

New Adventure Travel's Caetano-bodied MAN City Smart OV63 XDE (338) wore all-over white, with NAT fleet names, in December 2013, prior to receiving fleet livery.

Stagecoach in South Wales Enviro200 MMC YX66 WJV (26107) is part of the initial Gold batch delivered to South Wales with this body type in 2016. The 2017 batch had white LED destination displays, adding noticeable variety to the Gold fleet. Wearing route branding for the 132 service, it heads towards Cardiff Bay from Pontypridd in June 2019.

Resting in Abergavenny bus station, in front of the ex-Red and White depot and Shillibeer Routemaster, is Stagecoach in South Wales' R792 DHB, repainted in the striped livery that it wore when delivered new in 1998 as 792. It carries national fleetnumber 20392 in this shot, but displays its original fleetnumber in preservation with the Cardiff Transport Preservation Group. It was the last Alexander PS body built and the last high floor saloon delivered to the Stagecoach group. It was presented to the CTPG by John Gould, the then MD of Stagecoach South Wales, in April 2015.

Arriving into Pontypridd bus station from Blackwood is Harris Coaches' Optare Solo YJ54 UXF. New to First Yorkshire as 53821, it passed to Tyrer of Nelson, prior to passing to Harris Coaches as their number 32. The elevated car park alongside the railway line at Pontypridd provides a perfect location to observe the various buses enter and leave the town's bus station.

Megabus-liveried Van Hool Astromega CN61 FBD (50242) pauses in Newport prior to finishing its journey from London to Cardiff during April 2013. The vehicle moved from South Wales to Stagecoach Western, where it received X76 route branding for use between Glasgow and Kilmarnock.

Stagecoach in South Wales' Alexander Dennis Enviro300 CN60 CVR (27697) is ready to operate the X24 service to Newport, for which the vehicle is branded, in February 2011. This batch replaced Alexander Dennis Darts on the X24 in 2006, and were since replaced by Gold Enviro specification Enviro300s in 2015.

The Plaxton Pointer-bodied Dennis Darts transferred to Stagecoach in South Wales from London and converted to single door include V126 MVX and V137 MVX. The layover arrangement of Merthyr Tydfil bus station permits simultaneous front and rear shots of vehicles of the same type. The former (34126) carries 'Go 2' branding for Merthyr Tydfil services, having been previously branded for the Mainline X24 service when based at Cwmbran. The latter (34137) was not wearing any route branding at the time of the shot, in February 2010.

A side profile of Stagecoach in South Wales' YY15 KGG (28734) Scania-engined Enviro300, painted into Traws Cymru livery for use on the T4/X4. Three from the batch received this livery from Stagecoach corporate livery; they were numbers 28733–28735. Upon the delivery of Volvo Evoras in mid-2019, they reverted back to Stagecoach corporate livery.

Seen in Cardiff bus station in January 2006, First Cymru's CV55 AFE (20364) wears excel X2 branding for the Porthcawl–Cardiff route. The vehicle later passed to First Midland Bluebird to service on express services in Scotland. The X2 was upgraded with Cymru Clipper branded Optare Versas in 2013.

First Cymru's YN57 BVY (20325) looking smart in the coaching fleet livery on the 100 service to Swansea in May 2015. In 2018, the vehicle would be registered S30FTR, previously worn by a Wright Streetcar in Swansea, and given dedicated route branding for the Swansea to Cardiff service, renumbered the X10 after the demise of the 100 Greyhound service.

Stagecoach in South Wales' ADL Enviro300 SN65 OEC (27284) prepares for its return trip to Newport on the X24 Gold service when nearly new, in December 2015. It is one of fifteen in this batch that were delivered new to Cwmbran depot.

First Cymru Transbus Pointer Dart CU03 BHW (42694), wearing Fabian Way Park and Ride livery, at the 2006 Swansea Transport Festival. In later life, the vehicle wore Thomas Bros. centenary livery and lost its fog lamps (an uncommon addition), seen in the front corner panels in this photograph.

Silverline Dennis Darts were on show at the Merthyr Tydfil Transport Show in 2006. The Marshall-bodied M509 VJO wears route branding for the 775 Merthyr Tydil to Swansea service, whereas N262 FLR wears similar branding for route 470. The former served with the Oxford Bus Company, the latter previously serving Driving Ambition, Hammersmith, when new.

A July 2006 shot of MCW Metrobus A897 SUL, in Cardiff Bay on the open-top city tour, yet showing branding for the South Coast tour, adding variety and intrigue to the city sightseeing scene. The vehicle was new to London General in closed-top form in 1983, and was one of two Metrobuses acquired by Red Bus, Cyprus, in December 2008.

Cardiff Bus Leyland Lynx J271 UDW (271), entering Cardiff bus station in July 2006. Sister J267 UDW is a resident of the Cardiff Transport Preservation Group, together with other Cardiff Lynxes. The Lynx was largely replaced by Plaxton Pointer-bodied SLF Dennis Darts and their Transbus/Alexander Dennis equivalents.

Cardiff Bus' Plaxton Super Pointer-bodied Dennis Dart SLF Y373 GAX on the Beacons Bike Bus service, B8, in September 2006, complete with bicycle trailer. Scania-engined Wright Solar CN58 FFT (767), in the Cardiff Bus fleet, later received a tow bar for the same purpose, yet the number of vehicles to receive trailers across all local bus fleets in South Wales remains in single digits.

Part open-top Ayats Bravo-bodied Volvo B7L EU05 VBT is seen picking up in Cardiff Bay, when only a year old in 2006. RATP-owned Bath Bus Company rebranded the Cardiff Sightseeing Tour under the Navigatours name in May 2017, with similar EU05 VBO being the first to receive the new livery.

Second-hand MAN-engined Optare Vectas were purchased to update the Islwyn Borough Transport fleet in 2001. TIL 5405–08 (formerly P105–6 CPJ, P107–8 OPX) came from Tillinbgourne, Sussex, whilst N812–3 XJH came from Reading Transport. Ex-Tillingbourne example TIL 5406 is seen still in Islwyn Borough Transport fleet livery but with the addition of Stagecoach fleetnumber 39826 in July 2010 after working a local school service.

Ex-Islwyn Borough Transport MCV Stirling AE04 PJV (23), showing Stagecoach fleetnumber 39619, in January 2010, shortly after takeover by the group. Sister vehicle AE04 PJU became 39618 in Stagecoach ownership. After life with Stagecoach, both passed to Cotswold Green of Nailsworth.

Former Stagecoach London 17341 and previously Selkent ALX400-bodied Dennis Trident X341 NNO leaves Pontypridd on service 202 in October 2013, in New Adventure Travel ownership, yet to receive fleetnames.

Rear shot of Newport Bus's Alexander Dennis Enviro200 YX11 AGY (304), in an all-over Christmas wrap, in December 2012. Christmas liveries always delight festive shoppers, and a few have been applied to various vehicles in the fleet over the years.

Volvo B7RLE Wright Eclipse Urban BK10 MGE leaves Newport whilst on loan with Stagecoach in South Wales, during March 2011. With fleet number 80013, it was used extensively by Stagecoach in West Scotland, as well as Merseyside. It has since served with National Express in Dundee, carrying fleet number 2031 and the names *Aleecia/Jayden/Millie Carlin*. Following behind is MAN-engined Wright Meridian CN60 FBL (105), from Newport Transport, allowing comparisons to be made between the earlier and latter Wright designs.

New to Truronian, First Cymru's Mini Pointer-bodied Dart WK06 AEF (43851) is seen on Grayfriars Road, about to depart on their 400 service to Gwaunmiskin, during March 2012. Sister vehicles WK06 AEE/FV were also used (43850–3). First Cymru would later pull out of running this service, leaving Edwards to be the indirect successor to Bebb's Travel. Edwards started operating their 400E in competition with Veolia Transport Cymru, who subsequently withdrew upon the closure of their Treforest depot.

A lot of variety in this June 2010 shot at Blackwood bus station. Dennis Dart MPD T602 DAX was new to Glyn Williams Travel in all-over silver, celebrating twenty-five years of operation in 1999. In Stagecoach in South Wales ownership, as their 33286, it shows a rear end advertisement for Plumb Wales. Former Marshall-bodied Dennis Dart demonstrator L416 PAR stands alongside in Harris Coaches ownership as their RIB8431 (24). In shot, leaving the bus station, is Islwyn Borough Transport's YN04 FKJ (21) with rear end advertisement for Roberts Estate Agents.

Scania-engined Wright Solar Cardiff Bus CN58 FFZ (761) is seen at the Barry Festival of Transport, in June 2010. It is, numerically, the first one of the small batch of seven identical vehicles within the Cardiff fleet, new in November 2008, with fleet numbers 761–767.

Contrasting Optare Solos in Merthyr Tydfil, in August 2012. CN05 KTP (47195), with 'Go 2' branding, passes newer Solo SR CN12 CXW (47821) at the bus station. Unfortunately, the digital destinations were not captured, a frustration that bus/coach photographers did not need to contend with in vehicles with older style roller blinds. 47195 was hit by a tree when in service with Cwmbran depot in January 2015.

GX54 AOR was one of three Transbus Pointer Darts with Sixty-Sixty Coaches of Merthyr Tydfil for use on the X43 service serving Abergavenny, Nevill Hall Hospital, Crickhowell, Brecon, Merthyr Tydfil and Cardiff. They were not with the traditional destination blinds as the digital versions were available. The three joined various step-entrance Dennis Darts in the Sixty-Sixty local bus fleet.

Optare Solo YJ54 UWZ, belonging to independent operator Abbey Cars, is seen in Abergavenny bus station in October 2012. It held personalised registration BEZ 9083 and a yellow livery with red skirt whilst with Farleigh Coaches of Hoo, Rochester.

An October 2013 shot of Stagecoach in South Wales' Wright Streetlite WF CN12 ASO (43007) on service 27 to Twyncarmel from Merthyr Tydfil bus station. In attempts to boost bus travel in the Valleys and explain how easy it is, 'superpowers are not needed to get on our low floor easy access buses' vinyls were applied. The vehicle is also displaying service numbers 25/26/27/33/35/37/38, all operated by the Merthyr depot.

Later passing to Country Bus of Heathfield, Devon, Optare Solo YJ06 YRC is seen towards the end of its journey from Chepstow on service 73 in June 2010, as well as the end of Veolia life in Wales. The Veolia roundel towards the rear had not been reapplied when the rear window required replacement.

New Adventure Travel's Plaxton Centro CN07 FTE, still wearing Veolia Transport Cymru's grey-based livery applied for their 'glider' service 400 (Talbot Green to Cardiff), passes sister vehicle CN07 FTA in full New Adventure Travel livery in September 2012. Both later passed to Crosville of Weston-Super-Mare.

Veolia Transport Cymru's MCV Evolution CN07 FSE, pictured in April 2011. It would later pass to New Adventure Travel on the collapse of Veolia and be repainted into their blue and white livery.

Ex-Plymouth Citybus 275 Mercedes-Benz 811D N275 PDV is operating for Glamorgan Bus as it leaves Caerphilly bus station during May 2011 on an evening tendered service. Glamorgan Bus had a varied fleet and ceased trading in March 2013.

Rear shot of New Adventure Travel's Caetano-bodied MAN City Smarts at Pontypridd bus station in June 2019. OV63 XDA had a Castle Bingo rear advert, albeit partly removed due to a window replacement. On Service 111 to Ty Rhiw, OU14 SVV has an all-over rear advert for Coley y Cymoedd. Without adverts, OU14 SXL was departing on the X38 to Bargoed via Nelson, Gelligaer and Gilfach Estate.

A February 2011 short of Veolia Transport Cyrmru's Optare Solos CN06 BXH and CN56 FDU (40251), both branded for the 'one hundred', both new to Bebb Travel. The former, being used on the 55 from Cardiff to Bryn Heulog (Pentwyn), passed to First Potteries as their 53155. The latter passed to Mulleys Motorways, of Bury Saint Edmunds, with other ex-Bebb's/Veolia Cymru Solos, such as CN54 HFC and CN06 BXJ.

Transbus Mini Pointer Dart GU52 HAX passed to Harris Coaches as their 29 from Coastal, Rye, as their 116. It is seen in Blackwood bus station in August 2011, shortly after transfer and awaiting repaint into fleet livery. GU52 HAO also passed to Harris to become their number 30 in the fleet. Alongside is Stagecoach in South Wales' T12 SBK, new to Swanbrook, Gloucester, but which spent its later life operating around the Welsh Valleys with Stagecoach.

Alexander PS-bodied B10M L307 PSC, wearing route livery for the Merthyr Tydfil town circular service 66, although the vinyl, in place of a destination screen, had been changed from displaying route 66 to the S80 Treharris to Cyfarthfa Retail Park. The vehicle belonged to VR Travel as their 106 when photographed in September 2011, but was new to Stagecoach Fife Scottish in 1993.

Berkhof Axial Volvo B12M FL02 ZXW was new in April 2002 to Ferris Coaches of Nantgarw. It is seen on rail replacement duties during October 2013.

Diamond Holidays were purchased by Edwards Coaches in January 2011, after the firm earlier went into administration. Setra S416GT-HD BK09 RLY was later painted into the Edwards fleet livery, although it retained Diamond's gold-based livery in this November 2012 shot. Following behind was Edward's native Setra S416GT-HD BK08 NJU, which later wore cherished registration N800 EDW.

First Cymru's Optare Versa YJ13 HLW (49304) is seen on Fitzhamon Embankment with the Principality Stadium behind, in November 2014. It is in Cymru Clipper livery and has branding for the 'Vale Express' X2 service linking Cardiff with Bridgend, Cowbridge and Porthcawl.

Mercedes-Benz Citaro BF60 OEZ, on trial with Newport Bus in August 2012. The vehicle was also operated by Edwards and, surprisingly, with Stagecoach in South Wales on the X24 (Newport–Blaenavon), in October 2011. In November 2013, Cardiff Bus had the vehicle for training drivers, prior to delivery of new Citaros for their own fleet.

Former Stagecoach Devon Dennis Dart N24 PWV, seen in Chepstow bus station in the ownership of Chepstow Classic Bus. It once carried a cherished former Southdown 'Queen Mary' registration, 403 DCD, and originally started life in Hong Kong. Note its air conditioning roof pod, uncommon to Dennis Darts native to Wales.

Stagecoach in South Wales displayed ex-Islwyn Borough Transport Optare Solo YJ05 XOS (47715) and Traws Cambria-liveried Optare Tempo YJ55 YGC (25103) at the 2011 Transport Festival at Merthyr Tydfil.

South Wales Buses in the Twenty-First Century

A line-up of non-standard Stagecoach vehicles at Blackwood bus station in July 2011. Ex-Islwyn Borough Transport Optare Vecta M957 VWY (39822) sits alongside P103 BDB (33093), new to Cooper, Dunkinfield, and ended up with another Stagecoach branch before being transferred to the South Wales fleet. On the right is Caetano Nimbus-bodied Dennis Dart X191 FOR (33291), new to Glyn Williams Travel.

Newly refurbished Newport Bus ALX400-bodied Dennis Trident V140 HTG (40), displayed alongside Longwell Green-bodied Leyland PD2 PDW 484, new in 1958, at the Merthyr Tydfil Festival of Transport in September 2011.

The new order of the day on the Traws Cymru network is Stagecoach in South Wales operated Volvo B8RLE MCV Evora BV19 LPE (21353), seen in Merthyr Tydfil, turning onto stand to complete a short working T4 service to Cardiff via Pontypridd when only a week old, in July 2019. These were the first to be operated by the Stagecoach Group.

Volvo B8RLE MCV Evora BV19 LRF (21354) stands alongside Wright Streetlite WF CN12 AWU (43001). 21354 took part in the road run to mark the fortieth anniversary of the Traws Cambria network.

South Wales Buses in the Twenty-First Century 89

The rear of BV19 LPN (21358), operated by Stagecoach in South Wales, showing its 'wander through Brecon' rear vinyls. Each one in the fleet displays a different rear in the same style. Standing alongside is YN15 KGP (28738) with a rear vinyl advertising the X4/T4 service offering applied to a number of vehicles in the same batch.

A September 2011 shot of Chalfont Coaches' National Express-liveried Van Hool Acron-bodied Volvo B12B(T) WA10 ENL, displaying its Welsh dragon vinyls on the side and rear. Other National Express-liveried vehicles to display Welsh identity include Caetano Levantes FJ56 OBO/PFK and FJ12 FXZ.

Seen further away from its home city than usual, Cardiff Bus Y373 GAX (373) is in Abergavenny bus station on the 'Beacons Bike Bus' B8 service, operating from Cardiff to Brecon in early September 2006, pulling its bike trailer.

New Adventure Travel Optare Solo SRs YJ18 DHF, on service 105 to Dan y Lan, and sister vehicle YJ18 DHG, on the 103 service to Oaklands, in Pontypridd bus station, in June 2019.

The original seats in Cardiff Bus's Optare Olympus were replaced with these more lightweight versions, non-belted with orange top sections in keeping with colours of external livery. This is the interior of CN57 FGD (472).

The interior of one of Stagecoach in South Wales' Enviro300s, when new, for use on the X24. Route branding is evident on the side windows as well as Stagecoach specific advertising on the coving panels.

The top deck of Newport Transport's Enviro400 401. The Newport logo is pressed into the headrest of the batch. SN62 AOX (404) is unique as it has two tables on the top deck and was displayed at the 2012 EuroBus Expo at the NEC, Birmingham.

An interior shot of a Wright Solar-bodied Scania with Cardiff Bus. Note the cove panels displaying Cardiff Bus branding.

The interior of First Cymru's Wright Streetlite DF.

Interior shot from one of the first low floor batch of buses new to Stagecoach Red and White, Alexander-bodied Dennis Dart SLFs. 'Thank you for riding Stagecoach LoLiner' vinyls are evident on the coving panels at the front and lasted on the vehicles until withdrawal.

The interior of Glyn Williams Travel's HX51 LRZ in Stagecoach ownership in 2008. The vehicle would later receive a refurbished interior including Stagecoach moquette seats.

The interior of Alexander Dennis Enviro200 MMC YX17 NXA, on loan to Edwards, August 2017.

The initial interior of an articulated Cardiff Bus Scania Omnicity Baycar. BBC News 24 intervals displayed on the internal screens were a new feature for the fleet when the bus was new in 2006.

Infrequently used at the time of capture, in July 2014, the interior of Edwards Coaches' Plaxton Supreme IV-bodied Beford YMT JMA 880T was immaculately presented. The seat style, and retro colours and pattern of the moquette remind us of the way things once were in the bus and coach industry.

High backed grey seats with red piping on a Traws Cymru Optare Temp, operated by Stagecoach in South Wales. The digital display was used to give next stop announcements – a feature which has become more prevalent on Welsh vehicles over time.

Interior of a Traws Cymru MCV Evora, operated by Stagecoach in South Wales and complete with luggage racks. USB charging points are becoming more commonplace on new buses.

The interior of one of the Neoplan Starliners with Edwards Coaches, PK62 VUX. Perfect for coach holidays with the tinted glazed sections above the main windows. Edwards' 'simply the best way to get away' slogan is evident on the rear window.

Interior of Edwards Coaches' high specification corporate hospitality Van Hool TDX21 Altano, WA14 DTZ, complete with rear kitchenette, tables and multicoloured mood lighting.